The Sky Is Falling

Characters in the play:

 Narrator

 Henny Penny

 Ducky Lucky

 Goosey Loosey

 Foxy Loxy

Narrator:
Henny Penny went
for a walk.
Something fell
on her head.

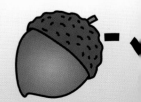

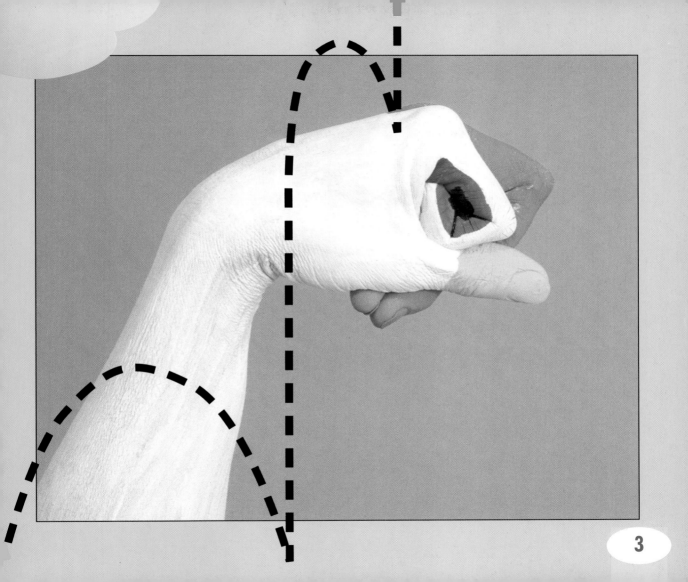

Henny Penny:
Oh no!
The sky is falling.
I will go
to see the king.

1.

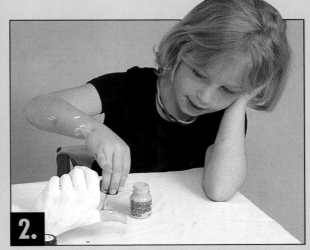

2.

3.

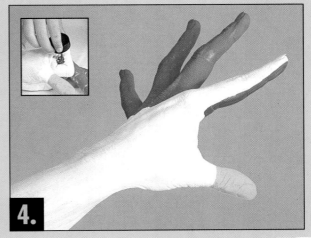

4.

Ducky Lucky:
Hello, Henny Penny.
Where are you going?

1.

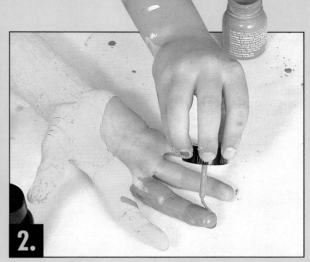

2.

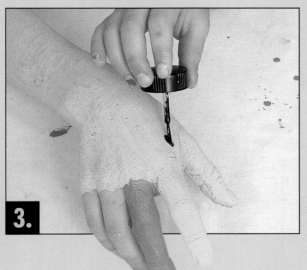

3.

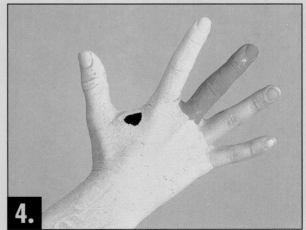

4.

Henny Penny:
I am going
to see the king.
The sky is falling.
A piece of it
fell on my head.

9

Ducky Lucky:
Oh no!
I will come with you.

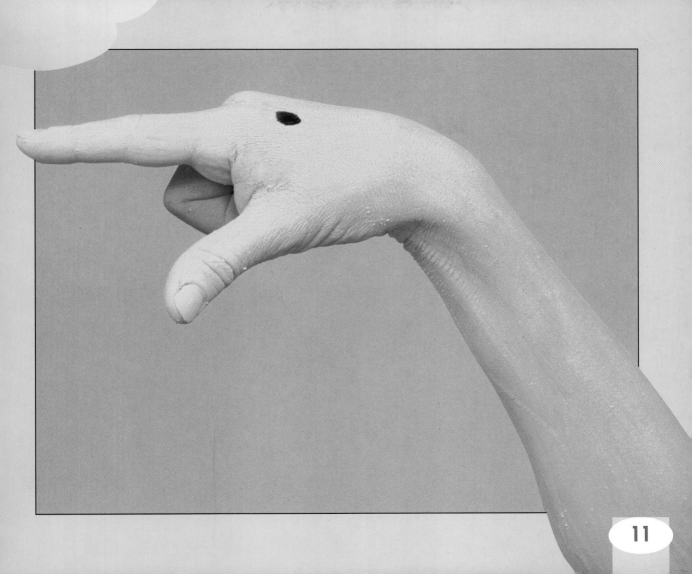

Goosey Loosey:
Hello, Henny Penny.
Hello, Ducky Lucky.
Where are you going?

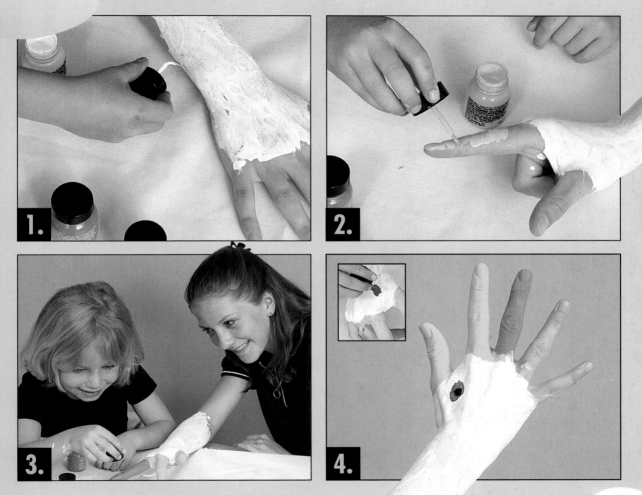

Ducky Lucky:
We are going
to see the king.
The sky is falling.

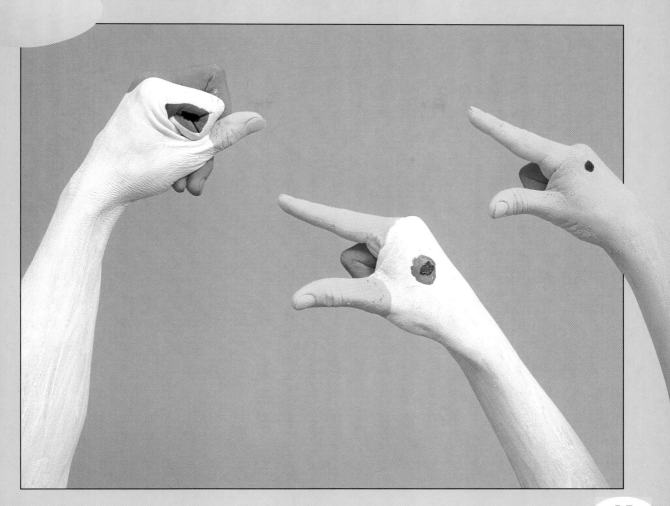

Henny Penny:
A piece of it
fell on my head.

Goosey Loosey:
Oh no!
I will come with you.

Foxy Loxy:
Hello, Henny Penny.
Hello, Ducky Lucky.
Hello, Goosey Loosey.
Where are you going?

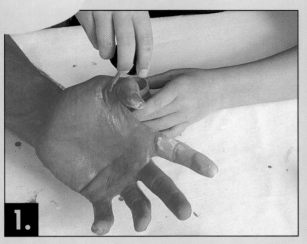

1.

2.

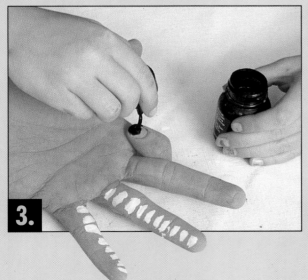

3.

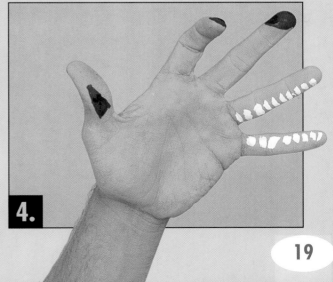

4.

Ducky Lucky:
We are going to see
the king.

Goosey Loosey:
The sky is falling.

Henny Penny:
A piece of it
fell on my head.

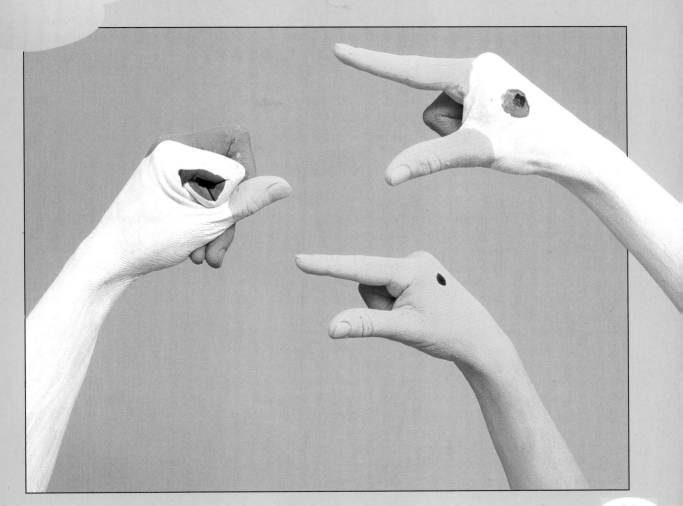

Foxy Loxy:
Oh no!
Come with me.
I will take you
to the king.

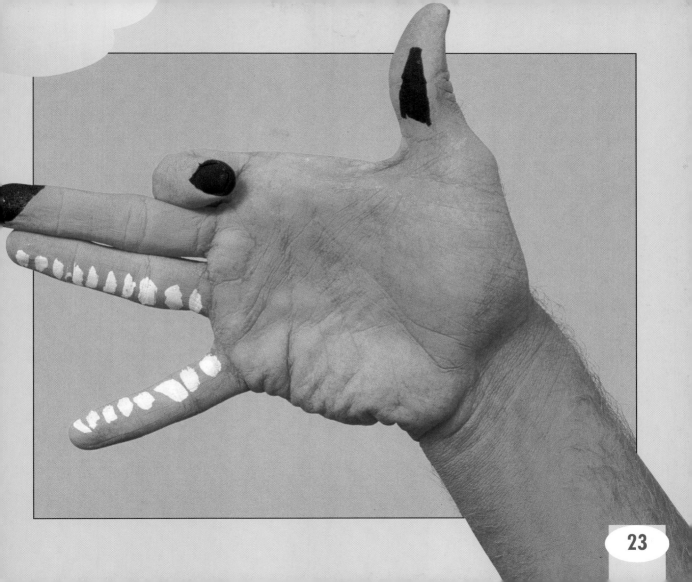

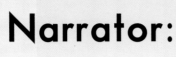

Narrator:
They went with
Foxy Loxy.
They did not
see the king.
They did not
come back.